QUICK QUIZZES

Presidents

By Rebecca Gómez

Cover photos:
AP/Wide World; The John F. Kennedy Library

Copyright © 2004 Kidsbooks, LLC
230 Fifth Avenue
New York, NY 10001

Manufactured in the United States of America

0804-1K

Visit us at www.kidsbooks.com

Contents

Introduction

Why are politicians in good shape? Because they're always *running* for office!

Are you a presidential scholar, or do you consider yourself a junior senator? If you've spent any time in a social studies or history class, you're bound to know something about U.S. presidents. You know, the people who run the country?

Test your political knowledge with this collection of puzzling presidential quizzes. Sharpen your pencil, furrow your brow, and get to work. Each quiz has a time limit, so get ready, get set, and go!

Presidential Firsts

Our past presidents have performed some very important firsts. Can you match the leader to his legacy? You've got 5 minutes and 10 questions. Good luck!

1. Which president was the first to be born an American citizen?
    (a) Martin Van Buren   (c) Lyndon B. Johnson
    (b) Bill Clinton   (d) George Washington

2. Which president was the first to visit Europe while in office?
    (a) Abraham Lincoln   (c) Dwight D. Eisenhower
    (b) John F. Kennedy   (d) Woodrow Wilson

3. Which president was the first to place a telephone call to the moon?
    (a) Thomas Jefferson   (c) Richard M. Nixon
    (b) Calvin Coolidge   (d) Theodore Roosevelt

4. Which president was the first to die while in office?
    (a) William Henry Harrison   (c) George Washington
    (b) Grover Cleveland   (d) Andrew Johnson

5. Which president was the first to use a telephone in the White House?
    (a) George W. Bush   (c) George Washington
    (b) George H. W. Bush   (d) Rutherford B. Hayes

6. Who was the first president to ride a train?
    (a) Jimmy Carter   (c) Benjamin Harrison
    (b) Gerald R. Ford   (d) Andrew Jackson

7. Which president was the first to travel underwater in a modern submarine?
    (a) Abraham Lincoln   (c) Harry S. Truman
    (b) Richard M. Nixon   (d) James Madison

8. Who was the first president to appear on television?
- (a) Grover Cleveland
- (b) Bill Clinton
- (c) George Washington
- (d) Franklin D. Roosevelt

9. Which president was the first to hold a press conference?
- (a) Ronald Reagan
- (b) John F. Kennedy
- (c) Woodrow Wilson
- (d) Martin Van Buren

10. Who was the first president to be born in a hospital?
- (a) Jimmy Carter
- (b) Herbert Hoover
- (c) George W. Bush
- (d) James Buchanan

Time's Up!

Click your stopwatch, then note your time: Did you make the cut? Check the answers below to find out how you scored.

How Did You Score?

1-4 Correct: *Beginner.* Maybe you need to pay a little more attention in history class.

5-7 Correct: *Intermediate.* Well done. You're not quite ready to be Commander in Chief, but you're on your way!

8-10 Correct: *Advanced.* Wow! Do you hear "Hail to the Chief" when you drift off to sleep at night? Check over your shoulder for a Secret Service detail.

Bonus! If you answered more than 7 questions correctly in under 3 minutes, you'd better start practicing your signature. You're going to be signing bills into law before you know it!

Answers:
1. a ('The seven prior presidents were born British subjects.) 2. d 3. c 4. a 5. d 6. d 7. c 8. d 9. c 10. a

Remember the Ladies

We've had some remarkable first ladies in our past. How much do you know about them? Test yourself with these toughies. You've got 5 minutes. Start the clock!

1. Which first lady was responsible for planting thousands of Japanese cherry trees in Washington, D.C.?
- (a) Laura Bush
- (b) Barbara Bush
- (c) Martha Washington
- (d) Helen Herron Taft

2. Who was the first first lady to be referred to as a First Lady?
- (a) Jacqueline Kennedy
- (b) Hillary Rodham Clinton
- (c) Eleanor Roosevelt
- (d) Lucy Webb Hayes

3. Which first lady was referred to as "Mrs. President"?
- (a) Edith Wilson
- (b) Nancy Reagan
- (c) Lou Hoover
- (d) Pat Nixon

4. Which first lady was well-known for her fashion sense?
- (a) Martha Washington
- (b) Mary Todd Lincoln
- (c) Eleanor Roosevelt
- (d) Jacqueline Kennedy

5. First Lady Nancy Reagan told children to "Just Say No" to what?
- (a) strangers   (b) drugs   (c) chocolate   (d) homework

6. Which first lady asked her husband to "remember the ladies"?
- (a) Hillary Rodham Clinton
- (b) Betty Ford
- (c) Abigail Adams
- (d) Lady Bird Johnson

7. Which first lady was called "Lemonade Lucy"?
- (a) Mamie Eisenhower
- (b) Lucy Hayes
- (c) Laura Bush
- (d) Abigail Adams

8. Which first lady was the first to live in the White House?
- (a) Mary Todd Lincoln
- (b) Abigail Adams
- (c) Laura Bush
- (d) Sarah Polk

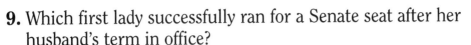

9. Which first lady successfully ran for a Senate seat after her husband's term in office?

    (a) Abigail Adams   (c) Hillary Rodham Clinton

    (b) Pat Nixon   (d) Nancy Reagan

10. Which first lady hosted the first Thanksgiving dinner at the White House?

    (a) Sarah Polk   (c) Dolly Madison

    (b) Betty Ford   (d) Martha Washington

Time's Up!

Click your stopwatch, then note your time: Did you make the cut? Check the answers below to find out how you scored.

How Did You Score?

1-4 Correct: *Amateur.* Whoops! If you want to learn about the first ladies, better study up!

5-7 Correct: *Semi-pro.* You seem to know your way around the female side of the White House.

8-10 Correct: *Professional.* Great work! Have you or any member of your family been a president?

If you answered more than 8 questions correctly in under 3 minutes, you are a first-lady fanatic!

Time Served

Some presidents have served in the military, and some have served during war. You've got 4½ minutes to answer these 10 military-related questions.

1. Who was the only president to have been a prisoner of war?
  (a) Andrew Jackson
  (b) Ronald Reagan
  (c) Lyndon B. Johnson
  (d) Rutherford B. Hayes

2. Andrew Jackson, who was a major general in the War of 1812, had what removed from his arm while in office?
  (a) a tattoo
  (b) a sliver of wood
  (c) a bullet
  (d) a mole

3. What was one of Theodore Roosevelt's famous mottoes?
  (a) "Speak up."
  (b) "Speak out."
  (c) "Speak softly and carry a big stick."
  (d) "Speak loudly and carry a small stick."

4. What president went to Korea to help bring an end to the Korean War?
  (a) Dwight D. Eisenhower
  (b) Abraham Lincoln
  (c) George W. Bush
  (d) Ronald Reagan

5. Which president made the decision to drop atomic bombs on Japan during World War II?
  (a) James Madison
  (b) James Polk
  (c) Warren G. Harding
  (d) Harry S. Truman

6. Which president commanded a PT-boat during World War II?
  (a) John F. Kennedy
  (b) Gerald R. Ford
  (c) Benjamin Harrison
  (d) Andrew Jackson

7. Which president is a graduate of the U.S. Naval Academy?
  (a) Grover Cleveland
  (b) Jimmy Carter
  (c) Abraham Lincoln
  (d) Ulysses S. Grant

8. Which president said, "Ask not what your country can do for you, ask what you can do for your country"?
- (a) George W. Bush
- (b) Gerald R. Ford
- (c) John F. Kennedy
- (d) James K. Polk

9. Which president spent a very difficult winter as a commander of troops at Valley Forge?
- (a) George Washington
- (b) Rutherford B. Hayes
- (c) Andrew Jackson
- (d) Dwight D. Eisenhower

10. Who was president when World War I broke out in 1914?
- (a) Abraham Lincoln
- (b) Bill Clinton
- (c) Martin Van Buren
- (d) Woodrow Wilson

Time's Up!

Click your stopwatch, then note your time: Did you make the cut? Check the answers below to find out how you scored.

How Did You Score?

1-4 Correct: *Private.* Okay, maybe military history is not your thing. These were tough—take a break, then try again!

5-7 Correct: *Corporal.* You're not quite ready to lead the fleet, but you'll get there!

8-10 Correct: *General.* Way to go! Uncle Sam wants *you*!

 If you answered more than 7 questions correctly in under 3 minutes, you're a four-star general. Congrats!

Answers
1. a (Andrew Jackson was a POW at age 14, during the American Revolution.) 2. c (Another bullet remained lodged near his heart for the rest of his life.) 3. c 4. a (During Eisenhower's campaign, he promised to put an end to the Korean War if elected.) 5. d 6. a 7. b 8. c 9. a 10. d (At that time, Wilson urged the United States to remain neutral.)

Those Wacky Presidents

Yes, they are high office holders, but presidents are people, too. Can you answer these true-or-false questions in 4 ½ minutes? Good luck!

1. The *S* in Harry S. Truman's name stands for Stanley.

        True   False

2. William Howard Taft was the heaviest president in U.S. history, weighing more than 300 pounds.

        True   False

3. Jimmy Carter was the first president to report a UFO sighting.

        True   False

4. Ulysses S. Grant received a speeding ticket for driving his horse and buggy too fast.

        True   False

5. Bill Clinton loved jelly beans, so the White House purchased about 12 tons of them during his time in office.

        True   False

6. Abraham Lincoln has the most places named for him.

        True   False

7. Bill Clinton was the only president elected to two non-consecutive terms in office.

        True   False

8. George Washington had sets of false teeth that were made from lead, elephant tusks, cow and hippopotamus teeth, and human teeth.

        True   False

9. George Washington was never married.

True   False

10. Chester A. Arthur, the 21st president of the U.S., changed his pants several times a day.

True   False

Time's Up!

Click your stopwatch, then note your time: Did you make the cut? Check the answers below to find out how you scored.

How Did You Score?

1-4 Correct: *Commoner.* Better put on your thinking cap and try again!

5-7 Correct: *Prince.* Great work! You know a thing or two when it comes to the human side of presidents.

8-10 Correct: *King.* When the teacher was handing out presidential trivia, you were obviously first in line. Way to go!

Bonus! If you answered at least 7 questions correctly in under 2 minutes, you're a presidential trivia dynamo!

Answers

1. False (It stands for nothing. His parents couldn't decide between either of his grandfathers' names, Shippe and Solomon, so they just used an S.) **2. True 3. True** (Jimmy Carter filed an official UFO sighting report in 1973, while he was the governor of Georgia.) **4. True 5. False** (It was Ronald Reagan who loved jelly beans.) **6. False** (It is George Washington, who can claim 257 townships, 121 cities and towns, 33 counties, and 1 state.) **7. False** (It was Grover Cleveland, who was both the 22nd and 24th president.) **8. True 9. False** (James Buchanan, the 15th president of the U.S., was never married.) **10. True** (He had more than 80 pairs of pants!)

Strange But True

All of our presidents have been distinguished people. But even distinguished people have a care-free side. See how much you know. You've got 10 ticklers and 4 minutes. Start that stopwatch!

1. Whenever Herbert Hoover and his wife, Lou, didn't want to be overheard, in which language did they speak to each other?
    (a) Pig Latin   (b) Chinese   (c) English   (d) French

2. Franklin D. Roosevelt wouldn't sit at a table with 13 people, and he would never leave for a trip on a Friday, because he was what?
    (a) superstitious (b) picky (c) annoying (d) silly

3. Grover Cleveland was the only president to do what in the White House?
    (a) work   (b) sing   (c) get married   (d) make dinner

4. Franklin D. Roosevelt's favorite hobby was collecting stamps. He started collecting when he was 11, and by the end of his life, he had about how many?
    (a) 25   (b) 250   (c) 2,500   (d) 25,000

5. What did Jimmy Carter sell on the streets of Plains, Georgia, when he was growing up?
    (a) peanuts   (c) pencils
    (b) autographs   (d) ice-cream cones

6. While Gerald R. Ford was in law school, he made some extra money by doing what job?
    (a) gardening (b) modeling (c) surfing (d) singing

7. What did Bill Clinton play on national television during his 1992 presidential campaign?
    (a) the spoons   (c) the recorder
    (b) the saxophone   (d) the piano

8. What did Theodore Roosevelt like to do after a busy day at the White House?

    (a) nap   (c) play golf

    (b) smoke his pipe   (d) jog

9. Which president's daughter held her senior prom at the White House?

    (a) Bill Clinton   (c) Andrew Jackson

    (b) Gerald R. Ford   (d) Abraham Lincoln

10. James A. Garfield could write with both hands at the same time. To amuse his friends, what did he write?

    (a) horoscopes   (b) jokes   (c) word searches

    (d) Greek with one hand and Latin with the other

Time's Up!

Click your stopwatch, then note your time: Did you make the cut? Check the answers below to find out how you scored.

How Did You Score?

1-4 Correct: *Wacky.* These were odd questions, after all. But think of all the fun facts you now know!

5-7 Correct: *Wackier.* You held your own with this off-the-wall quiz. Good work!

8-10 Correct: *Wackiest.* Fabulous! Is your address 1600 Pennsylvania Avenue?

Bonus! If you got more than 8 questions correct in under 3 minutes, your Senate seat is secure.

Who's in Charge Here?

Almost all U.S. presidents can claim some significant event during their time in office. Do you know who did what? You've got 4 minutes!

1. Which president signed a bill making "The Star-Spangled Banner" the national anthem of the United States?

  (a) Herbert Hoover (c) James Madison
  (b) James K. Polk (d) Ronald Reagan

2. Who coined the phrase "of the people, by the people, and for the people"?

  (a) Bill Clinton (c) George Washington
  (b) Abraham Lincoln (d) Thomas Jefferson

3. In 1776, the Latin phrase *e pluribus unum* was suggested as the U.S. motto. What does it mean?

  (a) All for one and one for all. (c) Stand proud.
  (b) Out of many, one. (d) We rock.

4. What was the total cost when Thomas Jefferson bought the Louisiana Territory from France?

  (a) $8,000 (b) $27,000 (c) $15,000,000 (d) $55,000,000

5. Which food did Americans think was poisonous until Thomas Jefferson ate some?

  (a) cheeseburgers (c) potato chips
  (b) tomatoes (d) lima beans

6. Dwight D. Eisenhower signed the bill that created NASA. What does NASA stand for?

  (a) National Aeronautics and Space Administration
  (b) National Aeronautics and Space Association
  (c) National Association of Space Academics
  (d) National Association of Space and Adventure

7. Which president created Medicare and Medicaid to help people pay their medical bills?

    (a) Thomas Jefferson   (c) George W. Bush

    (b) Ronald Reagan   (d) Lyndon B. Johnson

8. Presidents started wearing bulletproof vests after which event?

    (a) an Olympic skeet-shooting contest

    (b) an attempted assassination of Ronald Reagan

    (c) the popularity of vests

    (d) the fall of the Berlin Wall

9. Who was president during the Lewis and Clark expedition?

    (a) Lewis and Clark   (c) John Adams

    (b) Richard M. Nixon   (d) Thomas Jefferson

10. Franklin D. Roosevelt was famous for devising what?

    (a) Deal-a-Meal   (c) the Raw Deal

    (b) the New Deal   (d) the Deal

Time's Up!

Click your stopwatch, then note your time: Did you make the cut? Check the answers below to find out how you scored.

How Did You Score?

1-4 Correct: *Still Learning.* Better luck next time!

5-7 Correct: *Second Best.* Good job.

8-10 Correct: *First Class.* You're an ace when it comes to presidential trivia!

Bonus! If you answered at least 7 questions correctly in under 2 minutes, you're a sure shot for the White House!

Politics as Usual?

Are you up for the fast pace of this true-or-false quiz? You've got just 3 ½ minutes and 10 questions. Pencils ready!

1. Theodore Roosevelt was the first president to win a Nobel Prize.

                True   False

2. George W. Bush wrote a Pulitzer Prize–winning book.

                True   False

3. "Good to the last drop," a phrase still used in ads for a brand of coffee, was coined by President Bill Clinton.

                True   False

4. Martin Van Buren, who was in office from 1837 to 1841, once received live tiger cubs as a gift.

                True   False

5. Calvin Coolidge claimed this odd assortment of pets (in addition to others): a wallaby, a bobcat, and a pygmy hippopotamus.

                True   False

6. Thomas Jefferson created the animal symbols of the two main U.S. political parties—the donkey for the Democratic Party and the elephant for the Republican Party.

                True   False

7. On July 4, 1776, the first official copies of the Declaration of Independence were printed. George Washington printed them.

                True   False

8. The Baby Ruth candy bar was named for a president's daughter.

True   False

9. Thomas Jefferson served the first French fries in America.

True   False

10. George W. Bush made his fortune in the gold-mining business.

True   False

Time's Up!

Click your stopwatch, then note your time: Did you make the cut? Check the answers below to find out how you scored.

How Did You Score?

1-4 Correct: *Junior Senator.* These were hard. Review the correct answers so you can become a wiz!

5-7 Correct: *Senior Senator.* Good work. There were some toughies here, and you handled them well.

8-10 Correct: *President.* Nothing gets by you, does it?

 If you answered more than 6 questions correctly in under 2 minutes, you deserve a ride in the presidential helicopter!

Answers

1. **True** (He was awarded the Nobel Peace Prize in 1906.) 2. **False** (It was John F. Kennedy, for his book *Profiles in Courage*.) 3. **False** (It was Theodore Roosevelt.) 4. **True** 5. **True** 6. **False** (It was Thomas Nast, who was a cartoonist.) 7. **False** (It was a man named John Dunlap. Twenty-four of his originals, know as the Dunlap Broadsides, are known to exist today. Two are in the Library of Congress.) 8. **True** (It is named for Ruth Cleveland, the daughter of President Grover Cleveland.) 9. **True** (Jefferson served them at his home, Monticello.) 10. **False** (It was Herbert Hoover.)

Red, White, and Blue All Over

A lot of work goes into running this country. How much do you know about the presidents? Test your smarts with these puzzlers. You've got 4 minutes, but these questions are tough!

1. How much money per year does the president make today?
  (a) $20,000 (b) $100,000 (c) $400,000 (d) $1,000,000

2. Which president was the first to use the Presidential Seal?
  (a) Bill Clinton
  (b) James Madison
  (c) Thomas Jefferson
  (d) Rutherford B. Hayes

3. What is the name of the play that Abraham Lincoln was watching when he was shot on April 14, 1865?
  (a) *Cats*
  (b) *Our American Cousin*
  (c) *Beauty and the Beast*
  (d) *Our Town*

4. Which president had the most children?
  (a) James Madison
  (b) Martin Van Buren
  (c) John Tyler
  (d) Gerald R. Ford

5. Which U.S. president was the tallest?
  (a) Abraham Lincoln
  (b) James Madison
  (c) Franklin D. Roosevelt
  (d) Jimmy Carter

6. Which president was the shortest?
  (a) Bill Clinton
  (b) James Madison
  (c) Theodore Roosevelt
  (d) James Monroe

7. What will you find on the ceiling of the Oval Office?
  (a) the Presidential Seal
  (b) a flag
  (c) stars
  (d) stripes

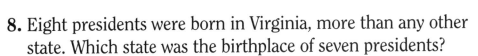

8. Eight presidents were born in Virginia, more than any other state. Which state was the birthplace of seven presidents?
    (a) Pennsylvania (b) Connecticut (c) Hawaii (d) Ohio

9. Ronald Reagan was the oldest man elected president. Who was the second-oldest?
    (a) Jimmy Carter   (c) William Henry Harrison
    (b) John Tyler   (d) Ulysses S. Grant

10. A little girl wrote a letter to Abraham Lincoln, suggesting that he would get more votes if he did what?
    (a) grew a beard   (c) played the guitar
    (b) outlawed dogs   (d) threw a big party

Time's Up!

Click your stopwatch, then note your time: Did you make the cut? Check the answers below to find out how you scored.

How Did You Score?

1-4 Correct: *Volunteer.* Oops! Did the stopwatch make you nervous?
5-7 Correct: *Intern.* Good job! Keep hitting the books and you'll ace these quizzes in no time.
8-10 Correct: *Staffer.* Wow! Are you the registrar of voters for your town?

 Bonus! If you answered more than 8 questions correctly in under 3 minutes, you're the cream of the crop!

Hail to the Chief

Have you ever thought about running for office? Whether you are treasurer of the chess club or president of the National Honor Society, holding office is a lot of work. How much do you know? You've only got 3 minutes to find out!

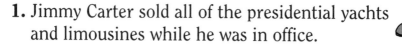

1. Jimmy Carter sold all of the presidential yachts and limousines while he was in office.

> True   False

2. When George Washington was president, slaves made up 50 percent of the U.S. population.

> True   False

3. During George Washington's presidency, census takers counted each slave as only three fifths of a person.

> True   False

4. James A. Garfield was only three years old when he learned to read.

> True   False

5. Richard M. Nixon was the first president to be impeached (charged with wrongdoing).

> True   False

6. Theodore Roosevelt wrote books on literature, history, hunting, the wilderness, America, and ranch life.

> True   False

7. John F. Kennedy was the youngest U.S. president to be elected to office.

> True   False

8. George H. W. Bush played the drums on a late-night television show.

True   False

9. Richard M. Nixon was the first and only U.S. president to resign.

True   False

10. Herbert Hoover lived and worked in China before becoming president of the United States.

True   False

Time's Up!

Click your stopwatch, then note your time: Did you make the cut? Check the answers below to find out how you scored.

How Did You Score?

1-4 Correct: *Seed.* You've got a long way to grow!

5-7 Correct: *Sapling.* Nicely done.

8-10 Correct: *Mighty Oak.* Very impressive! You've got the presidents covered!

Bonus! If you answered more than 8 questions correctly in under 90 seconds, you just may be taking the oath of office one day!

Answers

1. True (Carter didn't think that the president should be treated differently from any other American.) **2. False** (Twenty percent of the U.S. population was made up of slaves.) **3. True 4. True 5. False** (It was Andrew Johnson, in 1868.) **6. True 7. True** (Kennedy was 43 years old when he was elected.) **8. False** (in 1992, Bill Clinton played the saxophone on *The Arsenio Hall Show*.) **9. True 10. True**

Past Presidents

How much do you really know about the people who once ran our country? You've got only 3 minutes to find 10 correct answers!

1. Which president was the first to use the current Presidential Seal?
 (a) George H. W. Bush   (c) John F. Kennedy
 (b) Gerald R. Ford   (d) Harry S. Truman

2. What is the name of the home and burial place of the first president, George Washington?
 (a) Washington Square   (c) Lincoln Center
 (b) Mount Vernon   (d) Jefferson Valley

3. Which president was nicknamed "the Red Fox of Kinderhook" and "the Little Magician"?
 (a) Jimmy Carter   (c) Abraham Lincoln
 (b) Martin Van Buren   (d) John Tyler

4. Which president was the first to travel outside of the United States while in office?
 (a) Richard M. Nixon   (c) John F. Kennedy
 (b) George Washington   (d) Theodore Roosevelt

5. Where did Theodore Roosevelt travel during his presidency?
 (a) Russia   (b) China   (c) Panama   (d) Australia

6. Which president kept a pet alligator in the East Room bathroom?
 (a) Gerald R. Ford   (c) John Quincy Adams
 (b) Theodore Roosevelt   (d) James Madison

7. Which president was the first to be photographed?
 (a) Ronald Reagan   (c) Lyndon B. Johnson
 (b) James K. Polk   (d) Franklin D. Roosevelt

8. Which president was the first to be photographed while taking office?
- (a) Theodore Roosevelt
- (b) Abraham Lincoln
- (c) John F. Kennedy
- (d) Martin Van Buren

9. Who is buried in Grant's tomb?
- (a) Ulysses S. Grant
- (b) Ulysses S. Grant's cat
- (c) Ulysses S. Grant's dog
- (d) no one

10. Which president was an actor before becoming president?
- (a) Abraham Lincoln
- (b) Ronald Reagan
- (c) Thomas Jefferson
- (d) Richard M. Nixon

Time's Up!

Click your stopwatch, then note your time: Did you make the cut? Check the answers below to find out how you scored.

How Did You Score?

1-4 Correct: *Historian-in-Training.* Dust off those history books and study up!

5-7 Correct: *Historian.* Nicely done!

8-10 Correct: *History Buff.* You sure do know your stuff!

Bonus! If you answered more than 7 questions correctly in under 90 seconds, perhaps you can earn some college credits with this quiz!

Answers

1. d (in 1945) **2. b** (Mount Vernon is now a national registered historic landmark.) **3. b 4. d 5. c** (to inspect work on the Panama Canal) **6. c 7. b** (Polk was photographed in 1849.) **8. b** (in 1861) **9. d** (Technically, no one is buried in Grant's Tomb. President Ulysses S. Grant and his wife, Julia Dent Grant, are entombed there, in stone coffins in an above-ground chamber. They are not buried underground.) **10. b**

23

Fact or Fiction?

If the walls of the White House could talk, what kind of stories do you think they would tell? Separate fact from fiction with these 10 questions. You've got 3 minutes to do your best!

1. Thomas Jefferson had a pet mockingbird that he trained to sing alongside him while he played the violin.

    Fact!   Fiction!

2. George Washington used to soak his wooden teeth in tree sap.

    Fact!   Fiction!

3. President William McKinley had a pet parrot that could whistle "Yankee Doodle Dandy."

    Fact!   Fiction!

4. President George W. Bush fainted briefly after choking on a pretzel while watching an American football game on television.

    Fact!   Fiction!

5. James K. Polk, the 11th U.S. president, was nicknamed "Yolk" by his peers.

    Fact!   Fiction!

6. Ronald Reagan starred opposite a chimp in the 1951 movie *Bedtime for Bonzo*.

    Fact!   Fiction!

7. Geraldine Ferraro was the first female president of the United States.

    Fact!   Fiction!

8. George Washington was paid $25,000 per year to be president.

Fact!   Fiction!

9. The Muppet Grover is named for the 22nd president, Grover Cleveland.

Fact!   Fiction!

10. President Harry S. Truman had a sign on his desk that read, "The Buck Stops Here."

Fact!   Fiction!

Time's Up!

Click your stopwatch, then note your time: Did you make the cut? Check the answers below to find out how you scored.

How Did You Score?

1-4 Correct: *Boondocks Dweller.* Study up and try again!

5-7 Correct: *Townie.* Nicely done. You're obviously interested in American history, and it shows!

8-10 Correct: *Big-City Slicker.* You are good! You may even know more than some elected officials.

Bonus! If you answered more than 6 questions correctly in under 90 seconds, you are a quiz wiz! Great work!

Answers

1. Fact! 2. Fiction! 3. Fact! 4. Fact! 5. Fiction! 6. Fact! (Reagan was an actor who starred in more than 50 movies before going into politics.) **7. Fiction!** (Ferraro ran for vice president in 1984, but lost. There has never been a female U.S. president.) **8. Fact! 9. Fiction! 10. Fact!** (It meant that he assumed all responsibilities for his job.)

Around the World

No country stands alone. The U.S. has helped and received help from many nations. Can you answer these questions correctly? This quiz is super-tough. You've got only 5 minutes to show your stuff!

1. George Washington had a close associate from France who fought with him in the Continental Army. Who was he?
- (a) Yves St. Laurent
- (b) Jacques Chirac
- (c) Tout le Monde
- (d) Marquis de Lafayette

2. Thomas Jefferson is credited with introducing waffles to the United States. Where did he learn how to make them?
- (a) England
- (b) Belgium
- (c) the Netherlands
- (d) Germany

3. Thomas Jefferson also brought macaroni to our country. Where did he pick up his love of pasta?
- (a) Italy
- (b) China
- (c) France
- (d) Mexico

4. In 1962, which president narrowly avoided war by settling the Cuban missile crisis?
- (a) Gerald R. Ford
- (b) Ronald Reagan
- (c) John F. Kennedy
- (d) Bill Clinton

5. What war was the first to involve countries from all over the world?
- (a) Revolutionary War
- (b) Civil War
- (c) World War I
- (d) Korean War

6. James Monroe delivered a speech in which he warned European nations against establishing more colonies in America. What do we call this speech?
- (a) the Geneva Convention
- (b) the Presidential Warning
- (c) the Treaty of Versailles
- (d) the Monroe Doctrine

7. Which president started the Peace Corps?
    (a) Bill Clinton
    (b) John F. Kennedy
    (c) Richard M. Nixon
    (d) Abraham Lincoln

8. Which president, who was in office during World War II, died just weeks before the surrender of Germany?
    (a) Abraham Lincoln
    (b) John Tyler
    (c) Franklin D. Roosevelt
    (d) Ronald Reagan

9. Which president served as the first provisional governor of the Florida territory?
    (a) James K. Polk
    (b) George H. W. Bush
    (c) Andrew Jackson
    (d) Thomas Jefferson

10. Which president signed the Tariff Act of 1883?
    (a) Chester A. Arthur
    (b) George Washington
    (c) Martin Van Buren
    (d) Lyndon B. Johnson

Time's Up!

Click your stopwatch, then note your time: Did you make the cut? Check the answers below to find out how you scored.

How Did You Score?

1-4 Correct: *Impeached.* If at first you don't succeed, try, try again!
5-7 Correct: *Elected.* Not too shabby. You're doing a very respectable job.
8-10 Correct: *Re-elected.* You may be named president-for-life!

If you answered at least 8 questions correctly in under 3 minutes, you are an international know-it-all! Great work!

More Firsts

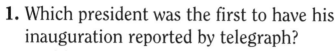

We've gathered up some more presidential firsts. You've got 2 ½ minutes. Good luck!

1. Which president was the first to have his inauguration reported by telegraph?
    (a) James K. Polk   (c) Thomas Jefferson
    (b) Abraham Lincoln   (d) George Washington

2. Which president was the first to speak over the radio?
    (a) John F. Kennedy   (c) Warren G. Harding
    (b) George W. Bush   (d) Rutherford B. Hayes

3. Who was our first and only Catholic president (as of 2004)?
    (a) Herbert Hoover   (c) Franklin D. Roosevelt
    (b) John Tyler   (d) John F. Kennedy

4. Who was the first former head of the Central Intelligence Agency (CIA) to become president?
    (a) George H. W. Bush   (c) Lyndon B. Johnson
    (b) Gerald R. Ford   (d) James Madison

5. During which president's term did Levi Strauss sell his first pair of blue jeans?
    (a) Bill Clinton   (c) Rutherford B. Hayes
    (b) John Tyler   (d) Ulysses S. Grant

6. Which president was the first to wear trousers regularly, instead of knee breeches?
    (a) Grover Cleveland   (c) Harry S. Truman
    (b) James Madison   (d) Ronald Reagan

7. Who was the first president to use campaign buttons?
    (a) Dwight D. Eisenhower   (c) William McKinley
    (b) Richard M. Nixon   (d) Martin Van Buren

8. Who was the first president to govern from coast to coast?
- (a) James Polk
- (b) George H. W. Bush
- (c) Thomas Jefferson
- (d) Millard Fillmore

9. During whose term was Coca-Cola first introduced in the U.S.?
- (a) Bill Clinton
- (b) Ronald Reagan
- (c) Grover Cleveland
- (d) Andrew Jackson

10. Which president started baseball's "seventh-inning stretch"?
- (a) Abraham Lincoln
- (b) Rutherford B. Hayes
- (c) William Howard Taft
- (d) George Washington

Time's Up!

Click your stopwatch, then note your time: Did you make the cut? Check the answers below to find out how you scored.

How Did You Score?

1-4 Correct: *Honorable Mention.* Wouldn't you like to win first prize? Study up and try again.

5-7 Correct: *First Runner-up.* You've got a good solid base; look over your answers to learn more.

8-10 Correct: *Winner!* Excellent work! Your knowledge is impressive!

Bonus! If you answered more than 7 questions correctly in under 90 seconds, you are presidential material!

Answers

1. a **2.** c **3.** d **4.** a **5.** d **6.** b **7.** c **8.** a (Polk also bought land from Mexico that later became California, New Mexico, Arizona, Utah, Nevada, and parts of Colorado and Wyoming.) **9.** c (Coca-Cola was first produced in Atlanta, Georgia, in 1886.) **10.** c (Taft stood up to stretch during the seventh inning of a baseball game. Other people stood, too, out of respect; then they realized it felt good to stretch!)

Did You Know?

You've got 10 toughies and only 2 ½ minutes. Are you up for it? Grab your watch and pencil and get ready to race!

1. Which president is connected with the teddy bear?
    (a) Warren G. Harding   (c) Franklin D. Roosevelt
    (b) Theodore Roosevelt   (d) John F. Kennedy

2. What was the connection between the president and the teddy bear?
    (a) He loved bears.   (c) He refused to shoot a bear.
    (b) He looked like a bear.   (d) He loved fur.

3. John F. Kennedy was killed during his presidential term. Who was held responsible for assassinating him?
    (a) Jack Ruby   (c) John Hinckley
    (b) Lee Harvey Oswald   (d) Sirhan Sirhan

4. Ronald Reagan survived an attack on his life in 1981. Who tried to assassinate him?
    (a) Lee Harvey Oswald   (c) Charles Manson
    (b) John Hinckley   (d) Jack Ruby

5. Who was the second president to be impeached?
    (a) Ronald Reagan   (c) Bill Clinton
    (b) John F. Kennedy   (d) Jimmy Carter

6. Which president had dreams of becoming a professional baseball player?
    (a) Bill Clinton   (c) Thomas Jefferson
    (b) George W. Bush   (d) William Henry Harrison

7. In 1929, which president told the nation that "Prosperity [economic growth] is right around the corner"?
    (a) James K. Polk   (c) James Madison
    (b) Herbert Hoover   (d) Thomas Jefferson

8. What was Benjamin Harrison so afraid of that he needed White House staffers to help him every day?

    (a) dogs   (b) bats   (c) electric lights   (d) water

9. When Bill Clinton was in high school, he shook hands with which president?

    (a) John F. Kennedy   (c) George Washington

    (b) Martin Van Buren   (d) Franklin D. Roosevelt

10. How many languages could Thomas Jefferson read?

    (a) 4   (b) 9   (c) 12   (d) 16

Time's Up!

Click your stopwatch, then note your time: Did you make the cut? Check the answers below to find out how you scored.

How Did You Score?

1-4 Correct: *Unsatisfactory.* Better hit those history books!

5-7 Correct: *Satisfactory.* Nice work!

8-10 Correct: *Excellent.* Wow! Your history teacher must be so proud!

Bonus! If you answered at least 6 questions correctly in under 90 seconds, your presidential limo awaits. Have a nice trip!

The Man, the Myth, the Legend

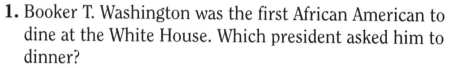

Can you answer these questions about some of our most important leaders? Hurry up. You've only got 2 minutes for this mind-bender!

1. Booker T. Washington was the first African American to dine at the White House. Which president asked him to dinner?

    (a) James Madison   (c) Theodore Roosevelt
    (b) Abraham Lincoln   (d) George Washington

2. Which president was the first to serve on the Supreme Court after his term as president?

    (a) Ronald Reagan   (c) John Tyler
    (b) Herbert Hoover   (d) William Howard Taft

3. Which president is considered a self-taught cowboy?

    (a) Theodore Roosevelt   (c) Harry S. Truman
    (b) Abraham Lincoln   (d) Bill Clinton

4. Which president helped build his family's log cabin?

    (a) Richard M. Nixon   (c) James K. Polk
    (b) Abraham Lincoln   (d) Gerald R. Ford

5. Which president was friends with Nathaniel Hawthorne, a famous author?

    (a) Jimmy Carter   (c) John Tyler
    (b) Martin Van Buren   (d) Franklin Pierce

6. When Ulysses S. Grant was five years old, what could he do?

    (a) speak Chinese   (c) long division
    (b) ride standing on horseback   (d) gymnastics

7. In 1964, the United States formally joined the Vietnam War. Who was president at that time?
- (a) Thomas Jefferson
- (b) Grover Cleveland
- (c) Lyndon B. Johnson
- (d) Ronald Reagan

8. Which president appears on the thousand-dollar bill?
- (a) George W. Bush
- (b) Harry S. Truman
- (c) Calvin Coolidge
- (d) Grover Cleveland

9. During whose term in office were 3-D movies invented?
- (a) George Washington
- (b) William Henry Harrison
- (c) Harry S. Truman
- (d) Bill Clinton

10. Who was the president in 1927, when Charles A. Lindbergh made the first solo airplane flight across the Atlantic Ocean?
- (a) George H. W. Bush
- (b) Calvin Coolidge
- (c) John F. Kennedy
- (d) Thomas Jefferson

Time's Up!

Click your stopwatch, then note your time: Did you make the cut? Check the answers below to find out how you scored.

How Did You Score?

1-4 Correct: *Fairy Tale.* This was a toughie, and time is getting tight. Better luck next time.
5-7 Correct: *Chapter Book.* Good job!
8-10 Correct: *Encyclopedia.* You know it all!

Bonus! If you answered more than 7 questions correctly in under 60 seconds, you should get busy choosing a running mate!

Still More Firsts

There have been more than 40 presidents, and all have been influential. There is bound to be tons of "firsts" to discover. How many do you know? Test your smarts with these 10 questions. You've got 2 minutes!

1. Which president was the first to receive a doctorate (a specialized degree)?
    (a) James Madison
    (b) Woodrow Wilson
    (c) Bill Clinton
    (d) William Henry Harrison

2. Which president was the first to have a Christmas tree in the White House?
    (a) George Washington
    (b) John Tyler
    (c) Benjamin Harrison
    (d) James K. Polk

3. Who was the first president to hire a woman to work in the White House?
    (a) Bill Clinton
    (b) James Madison
    (c) John F. Kennedy
    (d) Benjamin Harrison

4. Which president was the first to be defeated for re-election?
    (a) Abraham Lincoln
    (b) John F. Kennedy
    (c) John Adams
    (d) James A. Garfield

5. Which president was the first to die by assassination?
    (a) Abraham Lincoln
    (b) James Madison
    (c) Dwight D. Eisenhower
    (d) George H. W. Bush

6. Who was our first left-handed president?
    (a) Bill Clinton
    (b) James A. Garfield
    (c) Theodore Roosevelt
    (d) Franklin D. Roosevelt

7. Who was the first president to wear contact lenses?
- (a) Woodrow Wilson
- (b) Ronald Reagan
- (c) Jimmy Carter
- (d) Gerald R. Ford

8. Who was the first president born in the 20th century?
- (a) Martin Van Buren
- (b) Ulysses S. Grant
- (c) Dwight D. Eisenhower
- (d) John F. Kennedy

9. Who was the first sitting president to not seek reelection?
- (a) James K. Polk
- (b) James A. Garfield
- (c) Bill Clinton
- (d) George H. W. Bush

10. Who was the first president to govern 50 states?
- (a) George Washington
- (b) James Buchanan
- (c) Andrew Johnson
- (d) Dwight D. Eisenhower

Time's Up!

Click your stopwatch, then note your time: Did you make the cut? Check the answers below to find out how you scored.

How Did You Score?

1-4 Correct: *Rookie.* Back to the books!
5-7 Correct: *Semipro.* Not bad, not bad at all.
8-10 Correct: *Professional.* Wow! If there was a "Know Everything About the Presidents" league, you'd be in it!

Bonus! If you answered at least 7 questions correctly in under 60 seconds, you're the tops!

Answers
1. b (Wilson majored in political science.) **2. c 3. d** (Harrison hired a female clerk.) **4. c 5. a 6. b 7. b 8. d 9. a 10. d**

A Noble Calling

Can you whip through these brain busters in 2 minutes? Good luck!

1. Which president was buried wrapped in a U.S. flag with a copy of the Constitution beneath his head?
- (a) George Washington
- (b) Andrew Johnson
- (c) George W. Bush
- (d) Ronald Reagan

2. Which president was a Rhodes scholar?
- (a) Abraham Lincoln
- (b) James K. Polk
- (c) John F. Kennedy
- (d) Bill Clinton

3. Which president said, "The only thing we have to fear is fear itself"?
- (a) Bill Clinton
- (b) Jimmy Carter
- (c) Franklin D. Roosevelt
- (d) John Tyler

4. Which president was such an experienced speaker that he was able to deliver his inaugural speech from memory?
- (a) Dwight D. Eisenhower
- (b) Theodore Roosevelt
- (c) George H. W. Bush
- (d) Franklin Pierce

5. Where did Abraham Lincoln keep some of his important files?
(a) in his hat (b) in his shoes (c) in his car (d) in his pocket

6. Who was the only president to have a child born in the White House?
- (a) Jimmy Carter
- (b) Grover Cleveland
- (c) Warren G. Harding
- (d) Franklin Pierce

7. Who was the only president sworn into office on an airplane?
- (a) Lyndon B. Johnson
- (b) Richard M. Nixon
- (c) Theodore Roosevelt
- (d) Dwight D. Eisenhower

8. Who did George Washington call Sweetlips, Madam Moose, and True Love?
- (a) his wife
- (b) his horses
- (c) his dogs
- (d) his cabinet members

9. Which president, soon after his election, made the Cherokee and other Indian tribes leave their homelands in the South for reservations in the West?
- (a) Thomas Jefferson
- (b) Harry S. Truman
- (c) Andrew Jackson
- (d) Abraham Lincoln

10. Which president signed the 1850 Fugitive Slave Act?
- (a) Millard Fillmore
- (b) Rutherford B. Hayes
- (c) Ronald Reagan
- (d) Chester A. Arthur

Time's Up!

Click your stopwatch, then note your time: Did you make the cut? Check the answers below to find out how you scored.

How Did You Score?

1-4 Correct: *Third Place.* Time is tight—try again and you'll get more answers right!

5-7 Correct: *Second Place.* Good work.

8-10 Correct: *First Place.* Hats off to you!

 Bonus! If you answered more than 7 questions correctly in under 60 seconds, you are a trivia wonder!

On Whose Watch?

When judging a president's performance, it is important to understand the times during which he governed. How much do you think you know about this topic? Answer these 10 true-or-false toughies to find out. You've got just 1 ½ minutes!

1. During the term of Warren G. Harding, the U.S. population went over the 100-million mark for the first time.

True   False

2. During the administration of James Buchanan, the U.S. shrank in size.

True   False

3. William Henry Harrison was president when work began on the United States' first steam-powered railroad in Baltimore, Maryland.

True   False

4. William Howard Taft was president in 1912, when the *Titanic* sank.

True   False

5. In 1969, when Neil Armstrong became the first man to walk on the moon, Grover Cleveland was president.

True   False

6. Jimmy Carter was president when the first successful personal computer, Apple II, was introduced.

True   False

7. Franklin D. Roosevelt ran for president (and won) in 1932, during the Great Depression—the greatest economic crisis in U.S. history.

True   False

8. The Cold War was a war that was fought while Harry S. Truman was president.

True   False

9. William Howard Taft was the first president to have a presidential car.

True   False

10. Bill Clinton coined the famous phrase "A house divided against itself cannot stand."

True   False

Time's Up!

Click your stopwatch, then note your time: Did you make the cut? Check the answers below to find out how you scored.

How Did You Score?

1-4 Correct: *Grammar School.* Oops! Try again!

5-7 Correct: *Middle School.* You've got great potential! Keep hitting the books!

8-10 Correct: *High School.* You've done a fabulous job!

Bonus! If you answered at least 6 questions correctly in under 45 seconds, you should serve in Congress. The country needs you!

Answers

1. True 2. True (Slavery became such a big issue that South Carolina led six other Southern states to leave the Union in early 1861.) **3. False** (John Quincy Adams was president.) **4. True 5. False** (Richard M. Nixon was president.) **6. True 7. True 8. False** (Truman *was* president, but the "Cold War" wasn't a war. It was a competition between two types of government—democracy and communism.) **9. True 10. False** (It was Abraham Lincoln.)

Last-Chance Toughie

Okay, this is your last chance to show how much you know about the presidents. Have you learned all you need to answer these tough questions? We're giving you 8 minutes, but there are 20 questions. Are you ready? Then go to it!

1. Name two of the three presidents who have won the Nobel Peace Prize.

_____

_____

_____

2. Franklin D. Roosevelt was governor of New York from 1929 to 1933.

True   False

3. Which president came up with the idea of celebrating the Fourth of July with "games, sports, guns, bells, bonfires, and illuminations [fireworks]"?
- (a) John Adams
- (b) Andrew Jackson
- (c) James K. Polk
- (d) John F. Kennedy

4. George Washington wrote the Gettysburg Address.

True   False

5. Which president founded the Democratic Party?
    (a) Thomas Jefferson   (c) Franklin D. Roosevelt
    (b) Herbert Hoover   (d) Bill Clinton

6. Millard Fillmore established the first permanent library in the White House.

True   False

7. Which president was the first to appoint an African American to the U.S. Supreme Court? Who did he appoint?

_____

_____

8. Who was the only president not elected to either the vice presidency or the presidency?

   (a) John Adams
   (b) James Monroe
   (c) Gerald R. Ford
   (d) Bill Clinton

9. Millard Fillmore fell in love with his teacher and eventually married her.

True   False

10. On what day is Presidents' Day always celebrated?

_____

_____

11. George W. Bush is our 43rd president, but there have actually been only 42 presidents. Who was elected to two nonconsecutive terms?

_____

_____

$$\frac{C+T}{W^2X} \times \frac{\sqrt{\sqrt{M}}}{2} \times \sqrt{C>} = ?$$

12. Whose first lady taught him to write and do arithmetic?

    (a) George Washington   (c) Jimmy Carter

    (b) Andrew Johnson   (d) George W. Bush

13. What is the name of the person who assassinated Abraham Lincoln?

_____

_____

14. Jimmy Carter served the shortest time in office.

True   False

15. Franklin D. Roosevelt served the longest time in office.

True   False

Here are a few mix-and-match questions. Can you connect each question to the correct answer?

16. Under which president did the Thirteenth Amendment (which outlawed slavery) become law?

Benjamin Harrison

17. Which president helped pass the Virginia Statute of Religious Freedom, which allowed Americans to worship however they chose?

Andrew Johnson

18. Which president established the Antitrust Act, which forced big businesses to operate in a fair manner and be responsible to the public?

Zachary Taylor

19. During whose term did the California gold rush of 1849 begin?

Thomas Jefferson

20. During whose presidency was the first game of basketball played in 1891?

Theodore Roosevelt

Time's Up!

Click your stopwatch, then note your time: Did you make the cut? Check the answers below to find out how you scored.

How Did You Score?

1-5 Correct: *Class Clown.* Maybe you're more interested in mathematics?

6-10 Correct: *Class Secretary.* Excellent work. You should be very proud of yourself!

11-15 *Class Vice President.* You're giving the top dog a run for his money!

16-20 Correct: *Class President.* Why are you reading a book of quizzes? Don't you have a country to run?

Bonus! If you answered at least 15 questions correctly in under 4 minutes, we salute you. Hail to the Chief!

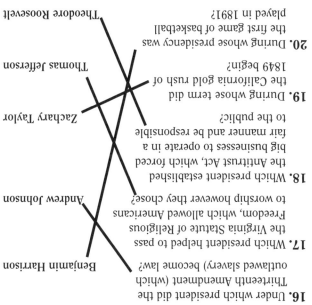

Theodore Roosevelt

Thomas Jefferson

Zachary Taylor

Andrew Johnson

Benjamin Harrison

16. Under which president did the Thirteenth Amendment (which outlawed slavery) become law?

17. Which president helped to pass the Virginia Statute of Religious Freedom, which allowed Americans to worship however they chose?

18. Which president established the Antitrust Act, which forced big businesses to operate in a fair manner and be responsible to the public?

19. During whose term did the California gold rush of 1849 begin?

20. During whose presidency was the first game of basketball played in 1891?

Answers

1. Theodore Roosevelt, Woodrow Wilson, and Jimmy Carter have won the Nobel Peace Prize. **2. True 3.** a **4. False 5.** a **6. True 7.** Lyndon B. Johnson; Johnson appointed Thurgood Marshall in 1967. **8.** c **9. True 10.** the 3rd Monday in February **11.** Grover Cleveland **12.** b **13.** John Wilkes Booth **14. False** (William Henry Harrison was in office just 32 days.) **15. True** (He was elected four times and was president for 12 years before dying in office at age 63.)

47

Presidential Roll Call

President	Years in Office	President	Years in Office
George Washington	1789-1797	Benjamin Harrison	1889-1893
John Adams	1797-1801	Grover Cleveland	1893-1897
Thomas Jefferson	1801-1809	William McKinley	1897-1901
James Madison	1809-1817	Theodore Roosevelt	1901-1909
James Monroe	1817-1825	William Howard Taft	1909-1913
John Quincy Adams	1825-1829	Woodrow Wilson	1913-1921
Andrew Jackson	1829-1837	Warren G. Harding	1921-1923
Martin Van Buren	1837-1841	Calvin Coolidge	1923-1929
William Henry Harrison	1841	Herbert Hoover	1929-1933
John Tyler	1841-1845	Franklin D. Roosevelt	1933-1945
James K. Polk	1845-1849	Harry S. Truman	1945-1953
Zachary Taylor	1849-1850	Dwight D. Eisenhower	1953-1961
Millard Fillmore	1850-1853	John F. Kennedy	1961-1963
Franklin Pierce	1853-1857	Lyndon B. Johnson	1963-1969
James Buchanan	1857-1861	Richard M. Nixon	1969-1974
Abraham Lincoln	1861-1865	Gerald R. Ford	1974-1977
Andrew Johnson	1865-1869	Jimmy Carter	1977-1981
Ulysses S. Grant	1869-1877	Ronald Reagan	1981-1989
Rutherford B. Hayes	1877-1881	George H. W. Bush	1989-1993
James A. Garfield	1881	William (Bill) J. Clinton	1993-2001
Chester A. Arthur	1881-1885	George W. Bush	2001-
Grover Cleveland	1885-1889		

(At the time of this printing, the 2004 presidential election had not taken place.)